THE UNIVERSAL BOARD HANDBOOK

Building Capacity Through Effective Governance

By
Dr. Victoria Boyd
President and Founder,
The Philantrepreneur Foundation

Copyright © 2025 Dr. Victoria Boyd

All rights reserved.

Published by The Philantrepreneur Foundation

No part of this publication may be reproduced, distributed, or transmitted in any form or by any means including photocopying, recording, or other electronic or mechanical methods—without prior written permission from the publisher, except in the case of brief quotations used in critical reviews and certain other noncommercial uses permitted by copyright law.

To order additional copies, access companion tools, or schedule training, visit:

https://BoardHandbook.PhilantrepreneurFoundation.org

For permission requests, write to:
The Philantrepreneur Foundation
Attention: Publications Department
marketing@PhilantrepreneurFoundation.org

Published in the United States by
The Galaxy Group, LLC
The Philantrepreneur Foundation
Nonprofit Capacity Through Education, Awareness, and Resources

ISBN: 978-0-9854219-6-0

Printed in the United States of America

TABLE OF CONTENTS

Section 1: Foundations & Orientation 1

    1.1 Message From the Philantrepreneur Foundation 2

    1.2 Why Capacity Building Is Central to Our Mission 2

    1.3 Building Organizational Capacity: The Essential Role of Every Board Member 3

    1.4 Understanding Board Roles and Responsibilities 4

    1.5 How This Handbook Is Organized 4

    1.6 Who This Handbook Is for and What It Is Not 5

    1.7 How to Use This Handbook 7

    1.8 Using the Personal Reflection Pages 7

    1.9 Your Commitment to Effective Governance 8

    1.10 Foundations of Nonprofit Governance 9

    1.11 Public Benefit Status and Stewardship 11

    1.12 Core Compliance Obligations 12

    1.13 Fiduciary Duties of Board Members 13

    1.14 Governance Accountability and Risk Oversight 14

    1.15 Mission Stewardship and the For-Purpose Mindset 14

    1.16 Measuring Mission Impact and Relevance 16

Section 2: Board Roles: What Every Board Member Represents 19

    2.1 Governance vs. Management 20

    2.2 Strategic Leadership 21

    2.3 Mission Stewardship 22

2.4 Ambassadorship and Representation 23

2.5 Continuous Learning as a Governance Role 23

2.6 Board Member Reality Check 24

2.7 A Strong Board Is Built On Intentional Commitment. 26

2.8 Serving Where You Thrive 26

2.9 Common Governance Myths: and the Truth Behind Them 29

Section 3: Board Responsibilities: What Every Board Member Must Do 33

3.1 Legal and Fiduciary Responsibilities 34

3.2 Oversight of Governing Documents and Policies ... 35

3.3 Financial Oversight and Stewardship 36

3.4 Transparency, Accountability, and Public Trust 36

3.5 Board Operations and Active Participation 37

3.6 Ethical Leadership and Decision-Making 38

3.7 The Board and Executive Partnership 38

3.8 Collective Responsibility and Decision Ownership 39

Section 4: Strengthening Board Performance & Accountability 41

4.1 Board Recruitment and Selection 42

4.2 Readiness and Board Integration 43

4.3 Term Limits, Rotation, and Succession Planning .. 44

4.4 Board Accountability and Engagement 46

4.5 Addressing Underperformance and Ethical Concerns 46

4.6 Evaluating Board and Individual Performance 47

4.7 Culture, Trust, and Shared Responsibility 48

4.8 Fundraising and Resource Development 48

4.9 Strategic Planning and Organizational Direction ... 49

4.10 Risk Management and Oversight 50

4.11 Governing in Times of Crisis 50

4.12 Technology, Innovation, and Modern Governance 51

4.13 Equity-Centered and Inclusive Governance 52

4.14 Community Accountability and Public Trust 52

4.15 Red Flags for Governance Breakdown 53

Section 5: Frameworks and Applied Governance 57

5.1 Governance Frameworks in Practice 59

5.2 Case Studies and Applied Examples 60

5.3 Board Reflection & Action 60

5.4 Closing Perspective 61

Section 6: Practical Tools for Governance in Action 63

6.1 Orientation Packet 64

6.2 Board Commitment & Acknowledgment 65

6.3 Meeting Tools 66

6.4 Financial Oversight Tools 69

6.6 Reflection and Action Worksheets 70

6.7 Using Tools Effectively 71

6.8 Continuing Your Governance Development 72

Section 1: Foundations & Orientation

1.1 Message from the Philantrepreneur Foundation

At The Philantrepreneur Foundation, we believe strong nonprofits are built on strong governance. Board members are not symbolic leaders or advisory figures; they are fiduciaries, stewards, and strategic partners entrusted with safeguarding mission, resources, and public trust.

The Universal Board Handbook was created to raise the standard of nonprofit governance by equipping board members with clear expectations, practical guidance, and shared language. This handbook is not designed to explain how one organization operates. Instead, it establishes universal governance principles that apply across nonprofit missions, sizes, and stages of growth.

Our commitment to capacity building is rooted in the belief that informed boards make better decisions, stronger organizations, and greater impact possible.

1.2 Why Capacity Building Is Central to Our Mission

Capacity building is the foundation of sustainable nonprofit success. Programs may change, funding may fluctuate, and leadership may transition, but governance capacity determines whether an organization can adapt and endure.

For board members, capacity building means:

- Understanding legal and fiduciary responsibilities
- Developing strategic leadership skills
- Strengthening financial literacy and oversight
- Embracing continuous learning and accountability

When boards invest in their own development, they move beyond compliance and into leadership. This handbook is one tool to support that evolution.

1.3 Building Organizational Capacity: The Essential Role of Every Board Member

Every board member contributes to organizational capacity through decisions made, questions asked, resources protected, and values upheld. Governance is not passive. It requires engagement, preparation, and a willingness to lead with integrity.

Board members collectively shape:

- Organizational direction and priorities
- Financial sustainability and risk tolerance
- Ethical standards and public trust
- Leadership stability and succession

This handbook establishes a shared foundation so all board members, regardless of background or tenure, understand what effective governance requires and how to contribute meaningfully.

1.4 Understanding Board Roles and Responsibilities

One of the most common governance challenges is confusion between roles and responsibilities. Roles describe what a board member represents and embodies. Responsibilities define what a board member must actively do.

This handbook intentionally separates these concepts to:

- Reduce micromanagement
- Clarify expectations
- Strengthen accountability
- Support productive board–executive relationships

Clear governance boundaries create space for both strategic leadership and operational excellence.

1.5 How This Handbook Is Organized

The Universal Board Handbook is structured as a progressive training and reference resource:

- Foundations of Nonprofit Governance establish the legal, ethical, and mission-centered context of board service.
- Board Roles explore what board members represent as stewards and leaders.
- Board Responsibilities define the core duties every board member must fulfill.
- Strengthening Board Performance addresses accountability, succession, and effectiveness.
- Advanced Governance & Practical Application provides tools, frameworks, and real-world guidance for modern boards.

Each section builds on the previous one, allowing boards to use this handbook sequentially or as a reference based on current needs.

1.6 Who This Handbook Is for and What It Is Not

This handbook is designed to support effective nonprofit governance by clarifying the roles, responsibilities, and expectations of board members and organizational leadership.

This Handbook Is For:

- Individuals currently serving on a nonprofit board of directors

- New and prospective board members seeking to understand governance expectations
- Board officers and committee chairs
- Executive directors and senior staff working in partnership with a governing board
- Organizations committed to strengthening board performance, accountability, and stewardship

The Universal Board Handbook is intended to be used as an educational and reference guide to promote sound governance practices and informed decision-making.

This Handbook Is Not:

- A substitute for an organization's bylaws or governing documents
- Legal, financial, or tax advice
- A one-size-fits-all policy manual for individual organizations
- A replacement for professional counsel or external facilitation when needed

Every nonprofit organization operates within its own legal, regulatory, and cultural context. While the principles in this handbook are widely applicable, boards are responsible for ensuring compliance with all applicable laws and for adopting policies and procedures appropriate to their organization.

1.7 How to Use This Handbook

This handbook is best used as:

- A foundation for board orientation and ongoing education
- A shared reference to clarify governance roles and boundaries
- A companion to an organization's bylaws, policies, and strategic discussions

When questions arise that extend beyond the scope of this handbook, boards should consult their bylaws, legal counsel, or qualified nonprofit professionals.

1.8 Using the Personal Reflection Pages

Throughout the handbook, you'll find Personal Reflection pages. These are intentional pauses designed to help board members connect governance concepts to their own experience, organization, and leadership style.

These pages are not tests — they are tools for clarity and growth.

Use them to:

- Identify where your board is strong — and where improvement is needed

- Capture questions to bring back to board discussions
- Reflect on how your role contributes to governance effectiveness
- Translate concepts into specific actions you can take

Take time to write honestly. Reflection deepens learning and creates accountability. Boards who work through these pages together often uncover insights that improve communication, alignment, and decision-making. Leaders may find it helpful to revisit these pages annually to track growth and identify emerging priorities.

With this framework in mind, the following sections introduce the core governance concepts every board member should understand.

1.9 Your Commitment to Effective Governance

Serving on a nonprofit board is a professional responsibility with legal, ethical, and public implications. By using this handbook, board members affirm a commitment to:

- Act in the best interest of the organization and its mission

- Uphold fiduciary and ethical standards
- Engage actively and prepare consistently
- Participate in continuous governance development

Effective governance is not achieved through intention alone—it is sustained through discipline, learning, and shared accountability. This handbook exists to support that commitment.

1.10 Foundations of Nonprofit Governance

Choosing the Right 501(c)(3): Public Charity vs. Private (Family) Foundation

While both public charities and private foundations fall under the 501(c)(3) designation, they are structured and regulated very differently. Understanding those differences helps organizations choose the model that best supports their mission, funding strategy, and level of community engagement.

Public Charities

Public charities are the most common type of 501(c)(3). They rely on **broad public support**, including gifts from individual donors, grants, events, and corporate partnerships. Because contributions come from many sources, public charities are expected to stay closely connected to the community and provide programs, services, or direct impact.

Key characteristics:

- Funding must come from a wide range of donors
- Eligible for most government and foundation grants
- Must demonstrate ongoing community benefit
- Typically, operated programs directly serving the public

This structure works best when the goal is **active programs, outreach, and community engagement**.

Private (Family) Foundations

Private foundations are usually funded by **a single source**. an individual, a family, or a business. Rather than running programs, most foundations provide grants to other nonprofits or fund specific initiatives that align with the donor's priorities.

Key characteristics:

- Limited funding sources (often one primary donor)
- Required to distribute a minimum amount each year

- Subject to stricter reporting and oversight
- Often focus on grantmaking instead of direct services

This model is ideal when the goal is philanthropic, giving with long-term control over how funds are used.

A Note on 501(c)(6) Organizations

Occasionally, groups discover that what they want to accomplish aligns more closely with a **trade association or business league**, classified as 501(c)(6). These organizations are not charitable and do not offer tax-deductible donations, but they allow greater flexibility in advocacy and member services.

Most mission-driven community organizations, however, will find that the 501(c)(3) structure best supports charitable work, grant eligibility, and public trust.

1.11 Public Benefit Status and Stewardship

A 501(c)(3) nonprofit is a public benefit organization. This means:

- The organization's assets are permanently dedicated to its charitable mission
- No individual may personally profit from the organization's earnings

- Upon dissolution, remaining assets must be transferred to another qualifying nonprofit

Board members are entrusted with oversight of these assets and must ensure they are used solely to advance the organization's mission. Stewardship is not symbolic; it is a legal and ethical responsibility.

1.12 Core Compliance Obligations

Maintaining 501(c)(3) status requires ongoing compliance at both the federal and state levels. Board members are responsible for ensuring systems and oversight are in place, even when day-to-day tasks are delegated to staff or external professionals.

Key compliance areas include:

- IRS Requirements: Filing an annual Form 990 to disclose financial activities, governance practices, and program impact
- State Filings: Maintaining good standing through required registrations and renewals with the Secretary of State and charitable solicitation agencies
- Restrictions on Political Activity: Prohibition of political campaigning and limitations on lobbying activities
- Public Transparency: Ensuring required documents are accessible and accurate

Failure to comply can result in penalties, reputational harm, or loss of tax-exempt status.

1.13 Fiduciary Duties of Board Members

Board members of nonprofit organizations are bound by three fundamental fiduciary duties. These duties apply regardless of board size, mission, or operating budget.

- *Duty of Care*: Actively participate in governance, make informed decisions, and exercise reasonable judgment in overseeing the organization's affairs
- *Duty of Loyalty*: Place the organization's interests above personal or professional interests and manage conflicts transparently
- *Duty of Obedience*: Ensure the organization complies with laws, regulations, and its own governing documents while remaining faithful to its mission

These duties form the legal backbone of board service and cannot be delegated away.

1.14 Governance Accountability and Risk Oversight

Boards are responsible for identifying, understanding, and mitigating organizational risks. This includes financial risk, legal risk, reputational risk, and mission risk.

Effective governance requires:

- Establishing and enforcing ethical standards
- Adopting and reviewing key governance policies
- Monitoring compliance and internal controls
- Asking informed, sometimes uncomfortable questions

Risk oversight is not about avoiding risk entirely, it is about ensuring risks are understood, intentionally, and aligned with mission and capacity.

1.15 Mission Stewardship and the 'For-Purpose' Mindset

Mission stewardship is the lens through which all board decisions should be made. A *for-purpose* mindset recognizes that while nonprofits exist to serve the public good, they must be governed with the same discipline, foresight, and accountability as well-run businesses.

The idea of 'for-purpose' leadership comes from a simple but often overlooked truth: philanthropy without strategy limits impact. Years ago, while teaching nonprofit management at UNLV, this principle surfaced repeatedly, *even in philanthropy, leaders must think like entrepreneurs*. Nonprofits may be mission-driven, but they still operate in environments shaped by competition, resource constraints, innovation, and performance expectations.

Nonprofits are exempt from taxes, not from responsibility.

This philosophy gave rise to the term Philantrepreneur, the belief that purpose and entrepreneurial thinking are not opposites, but partners. A for-purpose organization balances heart with discipline, values with viability, and vision with execution. It recognizes that sustainability strengthens mission, and strong governance makes impact possible.

Board members practice mission stewardship by:

- Governing with a long-term sustainability mindset
- Applying strategic thinking to mission advancement
- Asking how resources, systems, and leadership support impact
- Protecting the organization from mission drift *and* operational fragility

Strong governance does not diminish compassion, it reinforces it. When boards lead with a for-purpose mindset, good intentions are supported by sound decisions and lasting impact.

1.16 Measuring Mission Impact and Relevance

Boards are responsible for ensuring the organization's work remains meaningful and effective. This does not require board members to manage programs, but it does require them to understand outcomes and impact.

Effective boards:

- Review mission-aligned performance indicators
- Ask how success is defined and measured
- Use data to inform strategic decisions
- Adapt when community needs or conditions change

Impact measurement strengthens accountability to stakeholders and reinforces public trust.

Section 2: Board Roles: What Every Board Member Represents

Nonprofit boards exist to protect the mission, steward resources, and ensure the organization operates in the public's best interest. To do this well, board members must first understand *what governance truly is* and just as importantly, what it is not.

The following section clarifies the primary roles of a governing board and the essential boundaries that distinguish governance from management. Establishing this foundation creates clarity, reduces confusion, and strengthens the partnership between board leadership and staff.

Before examining responsibilities, it is essential to understand the role of a board member. Roles shape posture, mindset, and behavior. When board members misunderstand their role, even well-intentioned actions can undermine governance.

Board roles define how board members show up, not just what they do.

2.1 Governance vs. Management

One of the most persistent challenges in nonprofit governance is role confusion between boards and management. When boundaries blur, boards either disengage entirely or drift into operational control, both of which weaken the organization.

The board's role is governance. Management's role is execution.

Governance includes setting direction, establishing policies, ensuring accountability, and safeguarding mission and assets. Management includes leading staff, running programs, and implementing strategy.

Boards that respect this distinction:

- Focus on outcomes rather than tasks
- Hold leadership accountable without micromanaging
- Build trust instead of tension

Boards that do not often experience conflict, burnout, or leadership turnover, not because of bad intentions, but because of unclear roles.

2.2 Strategic Leadership

Board members are strategic leaders by design, not by title. Strategic leadership means governing with a long-term view while remaining responsive to current realities.

This includes:

- Protecting the organization's mission and vision
- Setting priorities that align with capacity and resources

- Asking questions that surface risk, opportunity, and alignment

Boards do not create strategy alone, but they are responsible for ensuring strategy exists, is realistic, and is monitored consistently. Without board-level strategic leadership, organizations drift from reactive decision to reactive decision.

2.3 Mission Stewardship

Every board member serves as a steward of the mission. Stewardship goes beyond belief in the mission, it requires active protection of purpose, relevance, and integrity.

Mission stewardship means:

- Evaluating decisions through a mission lens
- Preventing mission drift during growth or funding pressure
- Ensuring programs remain aligned with community needs

Boards that neglect stewardship may remain busy but lose relevance. Boards that steward mission intentionally ensure the organization's work remains meaningful and credible.

2.4 Ambassadorship and Representation

Board members represent the organization whether formally speaking on its behalf or not. Their credibility, conduct, and advocacy influence how the organization is perceived.

Effective board ambassadorship includes:

- Speaking accurately and consistently about the mission
- Building trust within professional and community networks
- Reinforcing organizational credibility

Ambassadorship is not marketing, it is governance in the public sphere.

2.5 Continuous Learning as a Governance Role

Effective governance requires learning. Laws change. Expectations evolve. Community needs shift. Boards that rely solely on experience become outdated.

Board members strengthen governance by:

- Participating in ongoing governance education
- Staying informed about sector trends and risks
- Reflecting on board effectiveness and growth

Learning is not optional, it is a governance responsibility.

2.6 Board Member Reality Check

Serving on a nonprofit board is both an honor and a serious commitment. Board members hold the ultimate responsibility for the organization's mission, assets, and reputation — even when day-to-day work is carried out by staff and volunteers.

Use the questions below as a personal reflection tool. They are designed to help prospective and current board members consider whether they are prepared to fulfill the expectations of effective governance.

Time and Presence

- Am I able to attend board meetings consistently and arrive prepared?
- Can I commit time between meetings to review materials, serve on committees, and follow up on assignments?
- Will I make board service one of my priority commitments during my term?

Responsibility and Stewardship

- Do I understand that board members have legal and fiduciary responsibilities, not just advisory roles?

- Am I willing to ask questions, seek clarification, and hold myself accountable for informed decisions?
- Can I put the organization's best interest ahead of personal preference or outside pressure?

Partnership and Governance
- Am I comfortable working as part of a collective decision-making body, even when I disagree?
- Do I understand the difference between governance and management — and am I willing to respect those boundaries?
- Am I prepared to support the executive director and staff while still maintaining appropriate oversight?

Advocacy and Support
- Am I willing to speak positively about the organization in the community?
- Will I participate in fundraising, relationship-building, and resource development in ways that align with my strengths?
- Can I model integrity, confidentiality, and professionalism as a representative of the organization?

2.7 A Strong Board Is Built on Intentional Commitment.

If these questions raise hesitation, it may indicate the need for additional training, clarity about expectations, or a conversation with board leadership. Effective governance is not about perfection — it is about willingness to learn, prepare, and actively engage in the work of stewardship.

2.8 Serving Where You Thrive

Effective board service is not just about filling a seat or matching a résumé to a committee. It is about contributing in ways that are meaningful, engaging, and sustainable.

Board members are most successful when they choose roles that align with their interests and motivation — not simply their professional expertise. Just because someone works in finance, marketing, health care, or law does **not** mean they must serve on the corresponding committee. Sometimes the work that feels most natural in a career can feel draining in board service.

Why This Matters

- People follow through more consistently when they care about the work

- Passion and curiosity often lead to stronger participation than obligation

- Committees benefit from diverse perspectives, not just technical specialists

- Board service should feel purposeful, not like "another job"

Questions to Consider

- Which committee topic genuinely interests me?

- Where do I feel energized and curious to learn more?

- Where will my time and enthusiasm have the greatest impact?

When board members serve in roles where they thrive, the entire organization benefits. Committees become more engaged, conversations become more thoughtful, and governance becomes more intentional. The goal is not simply to "fill positions," but to create an environment where each board member's contribution feels meaningful and valued.

Board Roles Personal Notes & Reflections

- How confident are you in distinguishing between governance and management in your current organization?
- What situations have blurred that boundary for you or your board in the past?
- What one step could you take at the next board meeting to strengthen clarity around roles?

Using the prompts use this space to capture thoughts. Consider how these concepts apply to your current or future board service.

_____
_____
_____
_____
_____
_____
_____
_____
_____
_____
_____
_____
_____
_____
_____
_____
_____
_____
_____
_____

2.9 Common Governance Myths: and the Truth Behind Them

Nonprofit board service comes with a lot of assumptions, most of them well-intentioned and often passed along informally. Unfortunately, some of these assumptions can quietly weaken governance and place the organization at risk. Understanding what myth is and what reality is helps a board make clearer, more confident decisions.

Even with clear responsibilities, misunderstandings about what boards should or should not be doing often arise. These misconceptions can unintentionally weaken governance or create tension between board and staff.

The next section addresses several common myths and replaces them with grounded, realistic expectations.

Myth 1: "Board Members Are Volunteers, So Expectations Should Be Flexible."

Reality:
Board members *are* volunteers, but they are also legally responsible for the organization. Serving as a volunteer does not reduce fiduciary, ethical, or governance obligations. Effective boards treat service as both a privilege **and** a professional-level commitment.

Myth 2: "The Executive Director Handles Compliance, The Board Just Supports."

Reality:
The executive director manages operations, but the board is ultimately responsible for ensuring legal and ethical compliance. Oversight, policy setting, financial accountability, and mission integrity remain governing responsibilities that cannot be delegated away.

Myth 3: "If the Board Agrees Unanimously, The Decision Must Be Right."

Reality:
Unanimity can sometimes signal healthy alignment, but it can also indicate lack of critical discussion, groupthink, or reluctance to disagree. Strong boards encourage respectful questions, alternative views, and thoughtful debate before making decisions.

Myth 4: "Fundraising Is the Job of the Development Staff, Not the Board."

Reality:
Staff may manage fundraising activities, but the board plays a vital role in supporting resource development. Board members serve as ambassadors, relationship builders, advocates, and when appropriate, donors. This

does not always mean asking for money, but it does mean helping secure resources that sustain the mission.

Myth 5: "Good Boards Stay Out of Difficult Conversations."

Reality:
Avoiding uncomfortable issues rarely protects the organization. Effective boards address challenges, performance concerns, financial questions, and mission drift directly while maintaining respect and professionalism. Courageous conversation is a core governance skill.

Myth 6: "Experience on Other Boards Automatically Makes Someone a Strong Board Member."

Reality:
Every organization has its own culture, bylaws, expectations, and needs. Prior board experience can be helpful, but it does not replace orientation, education, and alignment with the current organization's governance practices.

Recognizing myths is the first step in building stronger governance habits. When boards operate from clarity rather than assumption, they make better decisions, foster healthier relationships, and strengthen organizational trust.

Understanding board roles conceptually is only the first step. Effective governance requires thoughtful reflection about how each board member shows up, participates, and contributes.

Before moving forward into responsibilities and legal obligations, take a moment to consider your readiness for board service and how you can best contribute in ways that are both meaningful and sustainable.

Section 3: Board Responsibilities: What Every Board Member Must Do

Board responsibilities are not optional, symbolic, or dependent on professional background. They are legal, ethical, and fiduciary obligations that apply equally to every board member.

This section moves from *what board members represent* to *what board members must actively do*. Clear responsibilities protect the mission, the organization, and the individuals who serve.

3.1 Legal and Fiduciary Responsibilities

Serving on a nonprofit board carries legal obligations that cannot be delegated away. While staff, committees, and advisors may support compliance, ultimate responsibility remains with the board.

Every board member is legally obligated to:

- Act in the best interest of the organization
- Exercise independent and informed judgment
- Uphold fiduciary duties of care, loyalty, and obedience

Fiduciary responsibility is not passive. It requires preparation, engagement, and the willingness to ask questions—even when doing so is uncomfortable.

Boards that misunderstand fiduciary responsibility often assume "someone else is handling it." Boards that understand it recognize that oversight cannot be outsourced.

3.2 Oversight of Governing Documents and Policies

Governing documents are not administrative paperwork they are governance tools. They establish authority, define boundaries, and protect the organization from risk.

Board responsibility includes:

- Adopting and periodically reviewing governing documents
- Ensuring policies are current, enforced, and understood
- Using policies as decision-making guides, not shelf documents

When boards ignore governing documents, decisions become inconsistent and risk increases. Strong boards use these documents as anchors during growth, conflict, and change.

3.3 Financial Oversight and Stewardship

Financial oversight is one of the board's most critical responsibilities. Board members are not expected to manage finances, but they are expected to understand them.

Effective financial governance means:

- Reviewing budgets and financial statements regularly
- Understanding cash flow, reserves, and sustainability
- Ensuring appropriate internal controls are in place
- Asking questions until financial information is clear

Boards that disengage from financial oversight place the organization and themselves at risk. Financial literacy is not optional; it is a governance requirement.

3.4 Transparency, Accountability, and Public Trust

Nonprofits operate with public trust. Board members are stewards of that trust and must ensure transparency, accuracy, and ethical conduct.

This responsibility includes:

- Reviewing and understanding the organization's Form 990
- Ensuring truthful reporting to donors and stakeholders
- Addressing concerns that could damage credibility

Reputation is an asset built over time and lost quickly. Boards play a central role in protecting it through consistent oversight and principled decision-making.

3.5 Board Operations and Active Participation

Board service is a working role, not an honorary one. Effective governance depends on informed participation and collective responsibility.

Board members are expected to:

- Attend meetings consistently
- Review materials in advance
- Participate actively in discussions and decisions
- Support board decisions once made

When participation declines, governance quality follows. Strong boards normalize preparation and engagement as part of board culture.

3.6 Ethical Leadership and Decision-Making

Board members set the ethical tone for the organization. Ethical leadership is not situational, it is foundational.

This includes:

- Modeling integrity and professionalism
- Avoiding personal benefit from board service
- Disclosing and managing conflicts of interest
- Making decisions that withstand public scrutiny

Boards that tolerate ethical shortcuts undermine mission credibility and organizational stability.

3.7 The Board and Executive Partnership

One of the board's most important responsibilities is cultivating a healthy, respectful partnership with the organization's executive leader.

This partnership is defined by:

- Clear roles and mutual accountability
- Regular communication and support
- Performance evaluation aligned with strategy
- Planning for leadership succession and continuity

Boards that either micromanage or disengage weaken leadership effectiveness. Boards that partner well strengthen organizational resilience.

3.8 Collective Responsibility and Decision Ownership

Boards govern collectively. Individual opinions matter, but once decisions are made, board members share responsibility for outcomes.

Collective governance requires:

- Respecting the decision-making process
- Avoiding undermining decisions outside the boardroom
- Supporting implementation even when views differ

Unity after decision-making reinforces trust, credibility, and effectiveness.

Personal Notes & Reflections

Practicing Fiduciary Leadership

- Which of the fiduciary duties: care, loyalty, or obedience, do you feel most confident applying?
- Which is most challenging for you, and why?
- How can you strengthen your understanding of the organization's finances or policies in the year ahead?

Use this space to capture thoughts. Consider how these concepts apply to your current or future board service.

Section 4: Strengthening Board Performance & Accountability

Strong governance is not static. Even capable, well-intentioned boards lose effectiveness over time without intentional renewal, evaluation, and accountability. This section focuses on how boards sustain high performance, address challenges before they become crises, and ensure leadership continuity.

Board effectiveness is not measured by longevity, prestige, or fundraising capacity alone. It is measured by behavior, engagement, and the quality of decisions over time.

4.1 Board Recruitment and Selection

High-performing boards are built intentionally, not opportunistically. Recruitment based solely on personal relationships, availability, or fundraising potential often leads to imbalance, disengagement, or unmet expectations.

Effective board recruitment begins with clarity:

- What skills, perspectives, and experiences does the organization need *now*?
- What governance gaps exist that limit effectiveness?
- What level of commitment is required for meaningful service?

Boards that recruit well:

- Align board composition with strategic priorities
- Communicate expectations before appointment
- Treat board service as a professional responsibility, not an honorary role

When recruitment is intentional, board members arrive prepared to contribute, not figure things out after the fact.

4.2 Readiness and Board Integration

While this handbook is not an organizational orientation, boards remain responsible for ensuring members are ready to govern effectively. Governance readiness goes beyond introductions and document sharing, it establishes confidence, clarity, and accountability.

Governance-ready board members:

- Understand fiduciary duties and legal obligations
- Know where governance ends and management begins
- Are familiar with financial health, risks, and strategy
- Can participate meaningfully in decision-making early on

Without governance readiness, boards rely on assumptions, defer critical oversight, or disengage entirely. Effective integration protects both the organization and the board member.

4.3 Term Limits, Rotation, and Succession Planning

Term limits and leadership rotation are not about removing effective leaders. They are about protecting the organization from dependency, stagnation, and concentrated authority.

Boards that avoid succession planning often face:

- Disruption during leadership transitions
- Power imbalances
- Loss of institutional knowledge
- Resistance to new perspectives

Mature boards view succession as a system, not a reaction. This includes developing future officers, documenting leadership roles, and planning transitions well in advance. Succession planning signals stability, not instability.

Personal Notes & Reflection Building a Stronger Board Together

- How might your board benefit from new skills, experiences, or perspectives?
- What qualities do you personally look for when recommending potential new members?
- How can you support leadership continuity and mentor future board leaders?
- Use this space to capture thoughts. Consider how these concepts apply to your current or future board service.

_____

_____

_____

_____

_____

_____

_____

_____

_____

_____

_____

_____

_____

_____

_____

_____

4.4 Board Accountability and Engagement

Accountability is a governance safeguard. Boards cannot expect accountability from staff or executives if they do not model it themselves.

Effective board accountability means:

- Clear expectations for attendance, preparation, and participation
- Shared responsibility for decision-making outcomes
- Willingness to address disengagement or avoidance

When accountability is ignored, disengagement spreads quietly. Addressing issues early preserves trust, reinforces standards, and strengthens board culture.

4.5 Addressing Underperformance and Ethical Concerns

Avoiding difficult conversations weakens governance faster than almost any other behavior. Underperformance and ethical concerns rarely resolve themselves.

Boards must be prepared to address:

- Chronic absenteeism or disengagement
- Breaches of confidentiality

- Conflicts of interest
- Conduct inconsistent with mission or values

Clear processes, documented expectations, and fair handling of concerns protect both the organization and individuals involved. Governance maturity is demonstrated by how boards handle discomfort, not how they avoid it.

4.6 Evaluating Board and Individual Performance

Evaluation is not about fault-finding, it is about improvement. Boards that embrace evaluation demonstrate confidence, transparency, and commitment to excellence.

Effective evaluation practices:

- Assess overall board performance regularly
- Review committee effectiveness and workload balance
- Encourage individual reflection and accountability
- Translate findings into training or improvement actions

Boards that resist evaluation often stagnate. Boards that use evaluation thoughtfully evolve.

4.7 Culture, Trust, and Shared Responsibility

Board culture is shaped by what is modeled, reinforced, and tolerated. High-performing boards cultivate cultures rooted in trust, respect, and shared ownership.

Strong board culture includes:

- Open, respectful dialogue
- Healthy debate without personal conflict
- Commitment to mission over individual agendas
- Collective responsibility for governance outcomes

Culture does not emerge by accident. It is built intentionally through leadership, accountability, and consistency.

4.8 Fundraising and Resource Development

Fundraising is often one of the most misunderstood aspects of board service. While boards are not responsible for executing fundraising campaigns, they are responsible for ensuring the organization has the resources required to fulfill its mission.

Effective board engagement in fundraising focuses on:

- Ensuring a clear and realistic resource development strategy exists

- Supporting leadership through advocacy and relationship-building
- Setting appropriate expectations for board participation

Board members serve as ambassadors, not just donors. Their credibility, networks, and willingness to champion the mission directly influence donor confidence and organizational sustainability.

Boards that clarify fundraising roles reduce anxiety, improve participation, and strengthen long-term resource development.

4.9 Strategic Planning and Organizational Direction

Strategic planning is a governance responsibility, not a one-time exercise. Boards are responsible for ensuring the organization has a clear direction, measurable goals, and a framework for decision-making.

Effective strategic governance includes:

- Participating in strategy development alongside leadership
- Ensuring plans align with mission, capacity, and community needs
- Monitoring progress and adjusting direction when necessary

Boards that treat strategic planning as static documents miss opportunities for growth and resilience. Strategy should be reviewed, tested, and refined as conditions change.

4.10 Risk Management and Oversight

Risk is inherent in nonprofit work. Boards are responsible for ensuring risks are understood, intentional, and aligned with mission and capacity.

Key areas of risk oversight include:

- Financial sustainability and cash flow
- Legal and regulatory compliance
- Reputational and brand integrity
- Program effectiveness and mission alignment

Effective boards do not avoid risk; they govern it thoughtfully. Asking difficult questions before problems arise is a hallmark of responsible governance.

4.11 Governing in Times of Crisis

Crises test governance systems more than any other circumstance. Whether financial, reputational, leadership-related, or external, boards must be prepared to lead calmly and decisively.

Strong crisis governance includes:

- Clarifying decision-making authority
- Supporting leadership without undermining operations
- Communicating transparently with stakeholders
- Keeping mission and long-term stability at the center

Boards that prepare for crisis in advance respond with confidence rather than confusion.

4.12 Technology, Innovation, and Modern Governance

Technology continues to reshape how nonprofits operate, fundraise, and communicate. Boards are responsible for ensuring technology supports mission effectiveness, data integrity, and ethical practices.

Modern governance requires boards to:

- Understand how technology affects operations and risk
- Support innovation without mission drift
- Ensure appropriate data protection and cybersecurity measures

Innovation guided by governance strengthens impact. Innovation without oversight increases risk.

4.13 Equity-Centered and Inclusive Governance

Effective governance reflects the communities' nonprofits service. Equity-centered governance recognizes that lived experience, diverse perspectives, and inclusive decision-making strengthen outcomes.

Boards committed to inclusive governance:

- Examine whose voices are represented and whose are missing
- Integrate equity into strategy and oversight
- Avoid performative approaches that lack accountability

Inclusion is not a separate initiative; it is a governance lens that shapes how decisions are made and evaluated.

4.14 Community Accountability and Public Trust

Nonprofits exist to serve the public interest. Boards are responsible for ensuring accountability to stakeholders, beneficiaries, donors, and the broader community.

Community accountability includes:

- Listening to feedback and responding thoughtfully
- Evaluating impact beyond internal metrics

- Maintaining transparency and ethical standards

Public trust is earned through consistent, principled governance, not messaging alone.

Even strong boards can experience drifting over time. Priorities shift, leadership changes, and familiarity sometimes leads to complacency.

Before moving into practical tools and frameworks, the following section highlights common warning signs that governance practices may be slipping. Recognizing these indicators early allows boards to address issues proactively rather than respond to crisis.

4.15 Red Flags for Governance Breakdown

Strong governance does not happen by accident. It is the result of thoughtful practices, clear expectations, and consistent accountability. When these elements begin to weaken, warning signs often appear long before a serious problem develops. Recognizing these early signals allows boards to respond proactively rather than react to crisis.

Below are common red flags that suggest governance may be drifting off course:

Board Engagement

- Chronic absenteeism or frequent last-minute cancellations
- Limited participation in discussion or decision-making
- A small number of members carrying most of the work

Decision-Making

- Meetings focused only on reports rather than strategy or oversight
- Decisions made outside of meetings by a few individuals
- Lack of documentation explaining why major decisions were made

Roles and Boundaries

- Board members becoming involved in day-to-day operations
- The executive director making governance-level decisions without board input
- Committees functioning independently without reporting back to the board

Financial Oversight

- Financial reports not reviewed regularly or clearly understood

- Delays in audits, filings, or financial disclosures
- Budget decisions driven by assumption rather than data

Leadership and Culture

- Avoidance of difficult conversations or unresolved conflict
- Over-reliance on one person (board chair, founder, or executive director)
- Resistance to training, evaluation, or new perspectives

What to Do When Red Flags Appear

Red flags are not accusations — they are indicators that something may need attention. Healthy boards respond by:

- Asking thoughtful questions
- Reviewing policies and procedures
- Seeking outside facilitation or expert guidance when necessary
- Re-establishing expectations and accountability

Addressing governance issues early protects the mission, the organization's reputation, and ultimately the community it serves.

With a clear understanding of board roles, responsibilities, and potential areas of concern, the next step is putting governance into practice.

Section 5 provides tools, frameworks, and guided applications that help boards translate principles into daily operations and decision-making. These resources are designed to support consistency, accountability, and ongoing improvement.

Section 5: Frameworks and Applied Governance

As nonprofit organizations grow in complexity, governance must evolve with them. Advanced governance does not mean overcomplicating board work, it means governing with foresight, adaptability, and an understanding of the broader environment in which nonprofits operate.

This section addresses how boards apply governance principles to real-world challenges, emerging expectations, and changing conditions while remaining grounded in mission and fiduciary responsibility.

Boards succeed when governance principles are applied consistently, rather than understood by theory alone. This section provides practical frameworks and examples to guide decision-making, strengthen accountability, and improve board performance over time.

Frameworks give boards a **repeatable approach** to:

- Assess strategic alignment and organizational priorities
- Evaluate risks and readiness
- Balance mission, resources, and capacity
- Make consistent, ethical, and timely decisions

Applied frameworks also:

- Provide a shared language across board members
- Reduce reactive or inconsistent decision-making

- Support onboarding and ongoing board development

5.1 Governance Frameworks in Practice

Frameworks help boards move from awareness to action. They allow the board to approach challenges methodically, rather than reactively. For example:

- **Strategic Alignment Framework:** Ensures board decisions support the mission and strategic plan.

- **Decision-Making Framework:** Encourages consideration of legal, ethical, and financial factors before acting.

- **Risk Assessment Framework:** Evaluates operational, financial, and reputational risk to guide priorities.

Why this matters: Boards that apply frameworks are more confident, deliberate, and consistent. Frameworks protect the organization, reinforce fiduciary responsibility, and create a foundation for long-term success.

5.2 Case Studies and Applied Examples

Learning is most effective when governance principles are applied to real-world situations. Case studies illustrate:

- Common governance challenges
- Consequences of inaction or misaligned decisions
- Options for alternative approaches
- Opportunities to strengthen collective judgment

Why this matters: Boards that reflect on applied examples anticipate challenges and make decisions aligned with mission, ethics, and organizational capacity.

5.3 Board Reflection & Action

Boards strengthen their governance when members intentionally reflect and plan. Reflection promotes learning, accountability, and practical application.

- Capture insights from meetings and discussions
- Identify action steps for personal and board-wide improvement
- Track questions or initiatives requiring follow-up

Tip: Reflection exercises can be revisited periodically as part of ongoing governance assessment.

5.4 Closing Perspective

Governance is not a one-size-fits-all practice. Every organization has unique strengths, challenges, and cultures. The frameworks and applied examples in this section are meant to guide, not dictate. Boards are encouraged to adapt these practices thoughtfully to their context, ensuring alignment with mission, structure, and local requirements.

When boards combine intention, commitment, and adaptable frameworks, they create an environment where leadership is consistent, decisions are strategic, and missions thrive.

Section 6: Practical Tools for Governance in Action

Boards succeed not just by understanding governance principles, but by having **practical tools** that make implementation consistent, efficient, and professional. This section provides actionable resources boards can use immediately, along with guidance on how to adapt them to their organization.

Many of the tools below are also included in **The Universal Board Handbook Toolkit**, a companion set of downloadable templates, worksheets, and forms. The Toolkit offers expanded versions of these tools, but all boards can use the handbook versions independently.

Important: Every organization is unique. Tools should be adapted thoughtfully to match your board's size, mission, culture, and governance context. They are guides, not prescriptive rules.

6.1 Orientation Packet

Purpose: Ensure new board members begin service with clarity, understanding, and confidence.

Why it matters:

- Provides a structured introduction to governance responsibilities
- Reduces onboarding time for leadership and staff
- Ensures alignment with the board's culture and expectations

- Strengthens fiduciary understanding from the outset

Orientation Checklist (Handbook version):

This condensed checklist helps orient new board members and can be adapted for your organization.

- Roles and responsibilities explained – THE UNIVERSAL BOARD HANDBOOK (fiduciary duties, committees, leadership structure)
- Governing documents provided and reviewed (bylaws, policies, articles of incorporation)
- Conflict of interest disclosure signed
- Financial overview reviewed (budget, reporting, reserves)
- Mission, strategy, and key initiatives introduced
- Mentor or point-of-contact assigned
- Initial reflection: "Why I Chose to Serve"

6.2 Board Commitment & Acknowledgment

Purpose: Formalizes expectations for board members regarding participation, ethics, and fiduciary responsibility.

Why it matters:

- Clarifies responsibilities from day one

- Reinforces accountability for attendance, preparation, and engagement
- Strengthens professionalism and cohesion
- Provides a reference point if expectations are not met

Sample Commitment Statement:

I commit to actively participate in board meetings, uphold the organization's mission, follow fiduciary and ethical responsibilities, and contribute to the board's success to the best of my abilities.

Boards can adapt the wording to reflect local legal requirements, culture, and priorities.

6.3 Meeting Tools

Purpose: Efficient, productive meetings are the backbone of effective governance.

Why they matter:
- Reduce time spent preparing meetings
- Promote consistency and clarity in agendas
- Ensure accurate records of decisions and follow-up actions
- Support regulatory and fiduciary accountability

Sample Agenda Template:

Meeting Agenda Outline (Using Robert's Rules of Order)

Introduction This agenda follows the principles of Robert's Rules of Order to ensure an orderly and productive meeting. Each section provides structure to promote participation, maintain focus, and support fair decision-making. Boards should review and customize agendas to reflect priorities, strategic goals, and culture.

I. Call to Order

- Chairperson calls the meeting to order at the scheduled time.
- Record the exact time meeting begins.

II. Roll Call / Attendance

- Secretary calls the roll of members.
- Confirm a quorum is present.

III. Approval of Minutes

- Review and approve the minutes from the previous meeting.
- Address any corrections or amendments.

IV. Reports of Officers, Boards, and Standing Committees

- President's report
- Treasurer's report (financials and updates)
- Reports from established committees

V. Reports of Special Committees

- Updates from temporary or ad hoc committees.
- Actions or recommendations presented for consideration.

VI. Special Orders

- Items specifically assigned to this meeting or required by bylaws (e.g., elections, policy changes).

VII. Unfinished Business and General Orders

- Address matters carried over from prior meetings.
- Review pending motions or topics previously postponed.

VIII. New Business

- Introduce new topics, proposals, or motions for discussion and vote.
- Encourage orderly debate and decision-making.

IX. Announcements

- Share upcoming events, deadlines, or organizational updates.

X. Adjournment

- Motion to adjourn and recorded vote.
- Note official adjournment time.

6.4 Financial Oversight Tools

Purpose: Boards have a fiduciary duty to monitor and protect organizational resources.

Why they matter:

- Provide a standard approach to reviewing budgets, financial reports, and audits
- Reduce risk of errors or oversight
- Support accountability and confidence in stewardship

Financial Checklist:

- Review monthly financial statements
- Confirm budget alignment with strategic plan
- Track reserves and cash flow
- Note any unusual transactions or trends
- Document questions or follow-up for leadership

6.5 Policy & Procedure Templates

Purpose: Consistent policies help boards govern effectively and protect the organization and its members.

Why they matter:

- Ensure decisions are guided by clear standards
- Protect the board and organization legally and ethically

- Clarify expectations for staff, volunteers, and board members

Boards should review and modify templates to reflect organizational context, legal requirements, and culture.

Toolkit resources include Conflict of Interest forms, Confidentiality agreements, and sample governance policies.

Beyond policies, boards benefit from reflection exercises that turn governance principles into actionable practice.

6.6 Reflection and Action Worksheets

Purpose: Practical governance relies on ongoing learning and self-assessment.

Why they matter:

- Capture insights and questions during meetings or training
- Encourage personal and collective growth
- Create accountability for follow-through on decisions

Sample Reflection Prompt:

After each board meeting, take 5–10 minutes to reflect: What worked well? What challenges surfaced? What can I personally do to strengthen governance next month?

This reflection prompt illustrates a strategy used throughout the handbook: exercises embedded in key sections help board members personalize the learning experience, apply governance principles to their role, and translate knowledge into action.

6.7 Using Tools Effectively

When integrated with reflection exercises and the frameworks in Section 5, these tools help boards act with intention, consistency, and accountability. To maximize practical tools:

1. **Review resources in context:** Match tools to your board's structure, size, and governance culture.

2. **Customize thoughtfully:** Adjust language, process, and format to fit your organization while retaining governance with intent.

3. **Integrate with Section 5 frameworks:** Apply tools alongside frameworks and examples to reinforce best practices.

4. **Update regularly:** Even handbook tools benefit from review and adaptation over time.

By using these tools strategically, boards can reduce administrative burden, maintain consistency, and focus on mission-critical leadership.

6.8 Continuing Your Governance Development

Governance is an evolving discipline. As your board grows, faces new challenges, and refines its leadership practices, ongoing learning and access to practical tools make the difference between good intentions and sustained excellence.

This handbook establishes the foundation, but continued growth is strengthened when boards:

- revisit key governance concepts together,
- use consistent tools and templates to support accountability, and
- engage in intentional training experiences that deepen shared understanding.

Companion resources, additional copies of this handbook, and facilitated training, both live and virtual, are available to support boards at every stage of development.

These options are designed to help organizations translate knowledge into practice, strengthen decision-making, and build lasting capacity.

To order additional copies, access companion tools, or review training options, visit: https://BoardHandbook.PhilantrepreneurFoundation.org

Strong governance is not a static achievement, it is a continual practice of learning, reflection, and intentional action. This handbook provides the principles, frameworks, and tools to guide you, but true impact comes from applying them thoughtfully in your organization. Revisit sections as needed, engage in reflection exercises, and use the sample tools to strengthen your board's effectiveness. By leading with purpose, clarity, and accountability, you contribute to a board culture that sustains your mission and advances lasting community impact.

www.ingramcontent.com/pod-product-compliance
Lightning Source LLC
Chambersburg PA
CBHW031428290426
44110CB00011B/578